How to Matrix
Kick Boxing

Al Case

AL CASE

QUALITY PRESS

For complete information on Matrixing the Martial Arts, go to: MonsterMartialArts.com

ISBN-13: 978-1512215465

ISBN-10: 1512215465

Copyright © 2015 by Alton H. Case

All rights reserved. No part of this book may be reproduced or transmitted in any form or by any means, electronic or mechanical, including photocopying, recording, or by any information storage and retrieval system, without the written permission of the author.

Table of Contents

	introduction	5
1	Punches	9
2	Power	11
3	Building Mucles	13
4	Aerobics	15
5	Bagwork	17
6	The Bag from Hell	18
7	The Jab	25
8	The Cross	27
9	Straight Punches	28
10	The Roundhouse	30
11	Spinning Backfist	31
12	Kicks	33
13	Snap Kicks	34
14	Roundhouse Kicks	35
15	Side Kicks	37
16	Spinning 'Pop' Kicks	39
17	Sweeps	40
18	Other Kicks	41
19	Blocking	42
20	Blocking Kicks	43
21	Basic Strategy	44
22	The Nine Responses	50
23	Matrix of Strikes	52
24	Matrix of Squares	56

25	Pass and Stop	58
26	Fighting Strategy	60
27	The Alley	64
28	The Clinch	66
29	The Tactic of Positioning	68
30	The Mirror Drill Expanded	69
31	The Types of Fighters	71
32	The Matrix	77
33	Changing Types of Fighters	78
34	Analysis of Fighters	80
35	Timing	88
36	What Time Is	90
37	More Drills	93
38	Controlling a Fight	95
39	The Overview	97
40	Conclusion	101
	About the Author	102

Introduction

I remember when Kickboxing started.

It started back about 1970.

I remember going to a Karate tournament, and there was this one fellow, a white belt, who had no control.

He would bow to his opponent, and when the ref said to start he would run across the ring and start hitting him.

This wasn't Karate!

Not Karate at all!

But the referees didn't stop him, they didn't tell him he had to know Karate to fight in a karate tournament. They just let him keep running across the ring and hitting the other guy.

And his instructor just nodded happily and kept whispering in his ear, told him not to worry about being disqualified, because then everybody knew he was the winner.

Huh.

And I think the fellow was, eventually, disqualified.

And he should have been. He didn't know Karate. Or, rather, the karate he knew had been learned in a boxing ring.

He didn't set and throw the reverse punch. He didn't practice the classical front kick. He didn't block or maneuver for position, he just waded in and…boxed.

That tournament was in 1968, as I recall. And there had been a few rumors in the martial arts mags about this 'kick boxing' thing.

Over the next few years it would become more pronounced, people would badmouth Karate as being not practical enough, a few kick boxing leagues would start up, and the thing was, though we knew it not, here to stay. Simply, it provided more crowd entertainment, and it jacked the students up, and it didn't require much in the way of knowing forms or techniques.

Basically, it was boxing with Karate kicks. Though, to call the kicks Karate was sad. They were more of a hybrid sort of kick, a kick developing as Americans figured out how to use them in the ring.

And I know some people will object at my description of kick boxing as a sport where you didn't have to know much, just hit and kick and the bag.

But that's the way it was back then.

Now it has changed.

Now the 'sweet science,' as it is called, of boxing has had more impact.

Martial Arts, with its thousand and one concepts have trickled down.

Now it is a sport with bite, and with strategy, and with tactics, and even the rudiments of techniques.

Mind you, it is still not polished...it doesn't focus on the alignment of the skeletal structure except in the most rudimentary way. And it has no forms. And the techniques are very basic.

But, combatively speaking, it is one of the most useful of sports, and it has progressed to the point where we can matrix it.

Matrixing is the first and only science of the martial arts. Interestingly, it will always be the only science. This is because science is based on the measurement of the universe, and what we are measuring here is the individual, the art, and the combat between two. These things can be definitely measured. will never be different, and thus, any other development of science must duplicate Matrixing, or be an extrapolation thereof..

Nowadays, to continue my original thread, the interest in kick boxing has dwindled a bit.

And here is the sequence of 'art,' historically speaking.

Boxing came into vogue over the past few hundred years. There was prize fighting, the Marquess of Queensberry rules, and if you didn't toe the line you weren't a man. And if you didn't come out to toe the line for the next round you were likely an unconscious man.

Then Karate hit, pumped up even further by the Bruce Lee phenomena. Boxing took a back seat.

But, like a child that won't stay unnoticed, it clamored to get back into the ring.

Hence, kick boxing. The kicks of Karate (or whatever) and boxing.

But, before kick boxing could really define itself, jujitsu came along, with the Gracies and the Octagon, and MMA replaced everything.

Well, not really replaced.

For people still study the ancient oriental arts, and kick boxing is a mainstay in the hymns of the US gladiatorial arena.

But MMA is the big daddy, and the other arts, though fervently followed, take a back seat in many a spectators minds.

And they (the spectators) say such things as: Ku-roddy don't work on the street. And: kick boxing is gud for loosing wait.

I know, people don't sound that stupid. At least, not all the time.

But the point is this: kick boxing is easy to train, and easy to pitch to the buying public, and as long as you give everybody double-sized gloves.

Lord knows we don't want to give out lite gloves. That might hurt.

But fat gloves or skinny, this book is designed to help those who have been abused by insufficient training methods. Hopefully those people will have the chance to consider those methods, and to bring them a little more up to date.

Kick boxing is, after all, pretty darned good on the street, and it's pretty good conditioning, and there are a lot of benefits that one should take note of.

Heck, somewhere between Karate and going to the ground you're going to find Kick boxing, and it's a good thing.

CHAPTER ONE
PUNCHES

People tend to make things complex. Thus, you have the cross, the jab, the counter, the straight shot, the rabbit punch, the hook, the uppercut, and so on.

But those are just a bunch of names for two main punches.

The two types of punches are the the circular punch and the straight punch.

If you punch straight to the chin with the lead hand it is called a jab. A straight line out and back quick.

If you throw a roundhouse, with either hand, it is called a circular punch.

A hook is a round punch.

A cross is a straight punch.

An uppercut is a round punch.

The spinning backlist is a circular punch.

And so on.

Straight or circular. The arm cannot move in any other type of fashion.

CHAPTER TWO
POWER

Before we go into the strikes further I want to discuss where the power comes from in kick boxing.

There is no talk of 'chi power' in kick boxing. No talk of mystical energy or that sort of thing.

Instead, the power comes from the muscles.

You build up the muscles with three main methods.

One, you do weight lifting or body calisthenics.

Two, you do aerobics, such as running or skip roping.

Three, you hit the bag.

I know, there are lots of other exercises, medicine balls and drills and all sorts of things.

But, these three things seem to be the mainstay.

We will deal with each in its own right.

Right now I want to emphasize something else.

In the martial arts the power comes form the Tan Tien (The One Point), a spot two inches below the navel.

In boxing the pros understand that power comes from the feet. You push off the ground, use the whole body, and all the muscles, and the energy comes through the shoulders.

the beginners, or amateurs, don't understand that, or can't make it happen.

At any rate, two different methods.

Which methods, to be honest, are somewhat opposed. And possibly a reason why there has been some 'awkwardness' and lack of grace in certain fighters.

After all, do you throw the power from the feet and around the shoulders? Or do you sink the weight and punch using the stance, from the tan tien?

And, how do you make the shift from one to the other? This, alone, is a rather massive contradiction in the sport. One with severe consequences.

That's okay. You think about it, adjust accordingly, look to other arts (I recommend Matrix Karate to understand the martial arts better) and do your best to resolve the situation.

CHAPTER THREE
BUILDING MUSCLE

Weight lifting is done with moderation, and for a simple reason. Weight lifting tends to increase bulk and mass.

If you are a professional you have to stay in your weight limit.

If you are a lady then you, likewise, have to stay in your weight limit.

So the weight lifting is geared down for strength, but without increasing muscle mass, unless you just happen to be one of those guys that like to bulk up. Heck, you're not in the ring, and a little bulk can stop a fight before it stops simply because you present the image. The key is to never let the image get in the way of your ability. After all, what good does it do to look good if your training methods have made you slower, or less effective in some manner.

Calisthenics are done with more verve.

Sit ups (crunches, etc.) harden the core. This enables you to take a punch, and the core is considered the center of physical motion by many.

I find it interesting that there is such attention on building the core. The core, for classical martial arts, is the housing for the tan tien (The One Point). The tan tien is the center for chi, or that mystical stuff the boxer types tend to eschew.

Push ups are good for the punching muscles.

And other calisthenics, dips, etc., build the body in other ways, and if they don't contribute to the motion of the punch, they at least harden the body to a strike.

CHAPTER FOUR
AEROBICS

Aerobics is king. You need power to punch, and to get punched, but aerobics is designed for late in the fight. It is the key to getting to the end.

Bruce Lee said 'Running is king.'

One of his preferred training methods was running.

I remember a rather long lived running back by the name of Jerry Rice. He was renowned for his long runs. During the off season he would churn out the miles, and when the season started he was injury resistant, and could dig deep during those brutal fourth quarters.

His training consisted of a rather brutal four mile hill, and, as a result, he had more fourth quarter catches than any other player in history.

He recalled other players being out of gas, and he was still fresh, and it all came from…running.

So running is king, and that brings us to aerobics.

Which brings us to skipping rope.

Jump rope is aerobic, and it also disciplines the jumper into timing. Timing that lasts even when you're tired.

And there are other forms of aerobics, such as biking.

But these two are the real deal.

Professional boxers say you should run a mile for every round you intend to last.

15 miles is a bit much, but five miles is what Bruce Lee used to do.

Alternate running days with skip rope days and you'll be able to keep your aerobic work outs intense and fun.

CHAPTER FIVE
BAG WORK

Hitting the bag is hard work.

It is not just weight lifting, but speed weight lifting done in explosive bursts of increased weight.

When you connect with the bag, especially the heavy bag, you are suddenly trying to lift a heavy object on the end of your fist.

Hard work.

For those of you who doubt, try hitting a heavy bag for fifteen minutes. It won't be long before the muscles are like rubber bands, the breathing is coming hard, and you're wondering where the nurse is.

The other bag work is speed bag work.

The speed bag is not heavy, but it is fast and continuous, and it won't be long before you lose your sense of timing.

So you have to hit the heavy bag, and get used to moving weighty objects around.

And you need the speed bag to better your timing.

And you need to understand that the punch that wastes the most energy, that saps a fighter the most, is the punch that misses.

It's true.

CHAPTER SIX
THE BAG FROM HELL!
(...and how to make it!)

The following article, long out of print, tells how to make the perfect kicking bag, if you've got the apples for it.

"Go on, Al, kick it!"

I was surrounded by a half dozen black belts, all from a rival school, and they were very curious to see what my abilities were.

To the side stood Bob, their instructor. He just smiled affably.

In front of me hung...'the bag.'

It looked normal, probably about seventy pounds, a little dirty from foot marks. Okay, no problem.

I took a stance, launched myself through the air, and side kicked the bag.

My side kick was my most powerful weapon, but this time it didn't do the job. I felt a dull thud travel up my leg, the bag moved about an inch, and I actually bounced off it.

While everybody in the garage looked down and smothered their snickers, I stared at the bag in shock.

The score: Bag--1. Al--0.

Okay, I was embarrassed, at least until I found out how the bag was made. Then I was proud that I had moved it even an inch, and hadn't even broken my foot!

The purpose of this article is to give you a better kick, by enabling you to make a better bag. Then, when you kick some unsuspecting bag, you won't be the one 'getting mugged!'

Before we start, let me point something out. When you kick a bag you are kicking 70 to 100 pounds. The body of a mugger, however, might weigh two hundred pounds plus. So, no matter how hard you work at kicking that seventy pound bag, you are training yourself to kick half as hard as you need to.

So you need a better bag.

Heck, Bruce Lee, rumor has it, had a monster of a bag. It was over three hundred pounds!

Now that's a bag!

And if a 300 pound mugger came around Bruce you can bet he would get three hundred pounds of butt whipped, and whipped good!

Got it? Do you understand that you need a better bag? Good. Here's how I made my first bag, and how you can progress past my efforts to a true 'Bag from Hell.'

It was about 1970. I had no money, and I wanted a bag. Heck, my weak and puny kicks were desperate for a bag.

So, I went down to the army surplus store and bought a duffel bag for two dollars. I then went to the local sawmill and asked if I could have some free sawdust.

They must have thought I was nuts, but they said yes.

So I went out and loaded my duffel bag with sawdust. And I loaded a couple more grocery sacks with the stuff, too.

I went home and grabbed the duffel bag by the top, lifted it, and dropped it. And lifted it and dropped it. And....

A couple of hours later the sawdust was lower in the bag, and I added a grocery bag more to the mix.

And, a couple of hours later, I added another sack of dust.

At last, the sawdust finally refusing to settle anymore, I hung the thing from the beams in my garage. I nailed a couple of two by fours to the supporting beams to make sure I wouldn't shake the roof down, and I checked the windows to make sure they weren't going to crack and break.

Zingo bingo, I had a kicking bag for a couple of bucks.

Over the months I used that bag until it began to come apart.

When the material began to come apart I took the thing down to a cobbler and had him sew it back together, with extra material.

And I repacked it twice: I put a garbage can liner in it the first time, and the second time I just repacked the whole duffel bag into another duffel bag!

It was a great bag. Especially considering the price.

While I was improving my kicks on my own, I was also practicing on the bag at my school, the Kang Duk Won (House for Espousing {bubbling forth} Virtue).

The bag that hung there was solid, reinforced every time the support straps broke, and looked like a real Frankenbag. We had kicked a variety of holes in the thing, and it had been to the cobbler time and time again.

One day, after trying to knock the not inconsiderable stuffings out of the bag, I got into a conversation with Bob concerning what was in the bag, and this led me to the fascinating subject of how he hand packed his own bags, and, at last, I found out what was in the bag that had once kicked my fanny .

Here is how Bob packed his bag.

He bought an empty kicking bag and he packed it with sawdust, the same as I had packed mine.

The bag became quite packed, but it never became heavy enough for him.

What he did to remedy this was pour in a cup of sand every week.

The sand filled in the spaces, as it settled to the bottom of the bag, and the bag became heavier and harder.

Finally, the bag was more sand than sawdust, and it provided for a mighty meat of a kick!

My instructor, however, was still not satisfied with the texture and weight of the thing.

So, he began to add a cup of water every week!

His first problem was the thing became wet. Well, yeah. But he thought the moisture would go away and leave a better packing. It didn't, it began to rot the bag.

So he lined the bag with plastic liner and repeated the whole darn process, and this time he added a glop of bleach to stop the thing from rotting.

Well, the thing was a bag, but it was...weird. It was hard, but...squishy. And here was where my instructor showed his genius.

Instead of continuing with his efforts to make the perfect bag, he tossed everything out and started from scratch..and here is how you make the perfect bag. Perfect texture, perfect weight, no rot, and built to make your kicks perfect, or else!

Get a stack of newspapers and cut them in circles, then simply pack them in the bag.

Oh my God! After all the endless hours of packing (well, I had built my muscles up a little bit) the solution had been something entirely different than sand or sawdust or anything else!

Newspapers!

And you can add some sand to fill in the cracks.

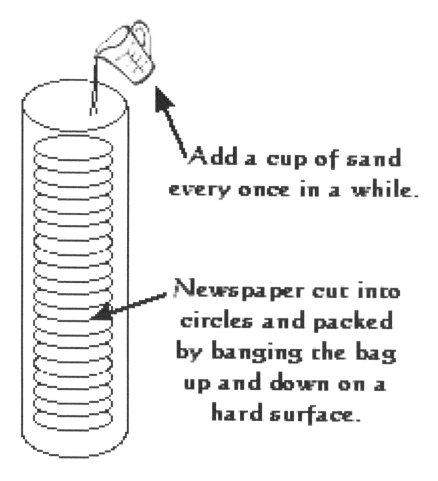

Add a cup of sand every once in a while.

Newspaper cut into circles and packed by banging the bag up and down on a hard surface.

I tell ya, a bag filled with packed newspapers is light enough so that you can still hang it from the rafters without making your whole garage sag, and yet provides a texture that is as hard as a bag of cement!

In short, all the news that is fit to print can provide you with the ultimate kicking bag, a 'Bag from Hell,' a bag that just might be 'too tough to kick.'

NOTE: The reader is warned, right now, that if you make such a bag you must be very careful. You hang such a monster at your own risk, and you kick such a beast at your own risk. The management will not be held responsible for injuries, either to the body, the roof, or the ego!

CHAPTER SEVEN
THE JAB

Now that you understand about power and such things, let's discuss a couple of things about the strikes.

The jab, for instance, is a lonely, little cuss. It is done off the front hand, usually with a quick spurt forward by the feet, with the lead hand. It goes for the chin.

Now, there are occasions when people knock other people out using the jab, but the truth of the matter is that it is a long distance, fragile thing, and the head is a shifty target, and it is usually used as a set up.

Jab, the opponent blinks, and you dig in the belly shot, robbing him of wind and setting up a massive haymaker which will remove said opponent's head from his shoulders.

And, that said, I recommend studying a little Jeet Kune Do.

JKD is Bruce Lee's art, and it proposes the jab as a full fledged fight ender. Though they are not so silly they would eschew any other strike, by itself or in any kind of combination.

Bruce studied fencing, and he modeled the jab on that rather than boxing, and so came up with some interesting concepts and drills and so on for developing and using the jab.

At any rate, Mr. Lee was QUITE thorough and in depth in assessing the jab, so I recommend examine his words and thoughts on the subject.

For a wonderful, little tome on advanced JKD I recommend a book called 'Bruce Lee vs Classical Martial Arts.'

CHAPTER EIGHT
THE CROSS

The cross is sort of a jab with the rear hand.

I know, that doesn't make a lot of sense, but it is a straight punch with the rear hand, and it tends to go in across the body a bit, and that makes it straight enough to be considered the rear hand equivalent of the jab. You just don't worry about snapping it as much as the jab.

Here's the thing: it establishes a line of reference for defining punches and strategy.

You are trying to establish a line from the fist to the point of the jaw (or other target).

You frequently have to go 'through' the opponent's arm.

So you set up the shot, and either go around (circular), or go inside (straight). Either way you may have to 'bully' his arm, even his own launched strike, out of the way.

So the idea is to point your fists at his shoulders. Have your own arms in the way of his strikes, and then shade inside or outside (right or left?), then override his strike.

And we come up with something interesting.

CHAPTER NINE
STRAIGHT PUNCHES

We are assuming he is striking with the same side arm you are. So your right arm has to deal with (go through) his left, and your left has to deal with (go through) his right.

If he throws a right straight punch and he is inside, then you have to shift so you are outside and left punch straight and override his punch.

If he throws a right straight punch and he is outside, then you have to shift so you are inside and left punch straight and override (from the inside) his punch.

And, you just reverse everything if he is punching with the left.

And, you can obviously set jab against jab, or jab against cross.

And it doesn't matter if he is punching with a lead (jab) or a cross. You simply keep your arms aligned with his arms, edge sideways to one side or the other, and develop a superior line of attack.

And if he doesn't set up, or sees it coming, simply back up. Give way and try again.

CHAPTER TWELVE
KICKS

One of the tools that suffered the most in the transition from Karate to Kick Boxing is kicks.

Specifically, I am referring to the tendency of fighters to throw a foot and not retract it, but to fall through.

This was considered incredibly sloppy technique.

The correct kick was to use the ball of the foot and actually strike a target, and then snap the foot all the way back to the ground.

And the people back then could do that.

It's more difficult, but take a look at Superfoot, and then revise your training so that instead of punching the bag mindlessly, you are doing thousands of kicks a day.

That's what it takes, and for most people that is a massive readjustment of your training schedule.

Kicks have just fallen out of vogue.

CHAPTER THIRTEEN
SNAP KICKS

This would be a straight kick, as opposed to a circular.

The mechanics of the kick indicate a certain circularity, but if you get the knee up and drive the foot forward on a line, then it works.

Problem: people don't like to get blocked.

Solution: train harder. Do more kicks. Examine the mechanics of the kick, of the leg, so that you better understand it.

The target is the belly. Or, on the street, the groin.

The reason this kick fell out of vogue was because people didn't study it hard enough to make it work.

They didn't bring the knee up, they tried to hurry it, they lost the focus, they couldn't beat the block.

And, to be honest, they weren't allowed the groin as a target.

Kick with the ball of the foot if possible, it has a smaller striking area, so you get more pounds per square inch.

CHAPTER FOURTEEN
ROUNDHOUSE KICKS

Roundhouse kicks, which my school called wheel kicks, are nothing more than snap kicks on the side.

But, even worse than the snap kick, they fell out of vogue.

People didn't practice enough to make them work, they didn't understand the mechanics, they didn't understand the importance of the ball of the foot (a smaller surface area for striking = more power to smaller target area).

And, to be honest, the impact of Muay Thai kicks was felt in American kick boxing.

Muay Thai likes to bludgeon thighs, as if with a baseball bat, or to kick a leg from the inside out.

As opposed to kicking somebody in the target with a precise 'balpeen hammer' of a ball of the foot kick.

So Muay Thai kicks were practiced, karate kicks were put by the side, and the real problem is that people weren't willing to do the thousands of kicks a day to make their kicks work.

The trick is to be able to use both kicks.

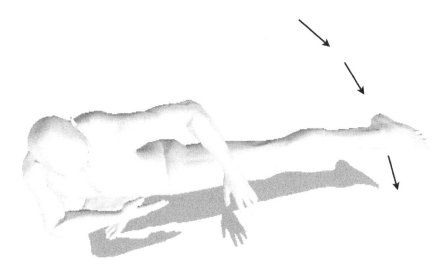

Kick comes in from the side, no body behind it, impact spread over larger area of instep.

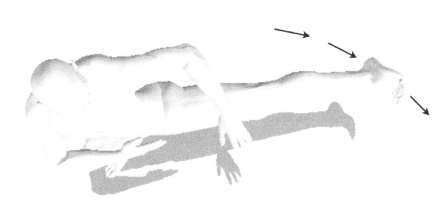

Kick comes in on a straighter line, body is behind it, can be snapped back, smaller striking area for more pounds per square inch.

CHAPTER FIFTEEN
SIDE KICKS

Same problem as the other kicks, but, in addition, in kickboxing, because there aren't stances as in Karate, such as the side stance, or horse stance, the body is not set up properly for the side kick.

Which is a shame, because if you make a slight step, as if you were going somewhere, you can fool a person into motion, and launch a side kick when they move to meet that motion.

The real problem, however, is that people don't understand that a side kick has to have a certain amount of focus, and this is sometimes difficult because the nature of the kick lends itself to power.

It is known as the most powerful kick, the whole body, including the turn of the hips, goes into the kick.

But that tends to slow it down, and people don't have the stances to set it up, and so...bye bye side kick.

Too bad, because it is a tremendous kick.

But, key to making it work, more practice.

And so many people figure they just don't have the time in their practice to spend on the drudgery of working on one tool forever. But that is the secret of success.

An arm in the wrong direction
is energy in the wrong direction,
which means you have to work harder
to balance the body, which means less
energy will go into the kick.

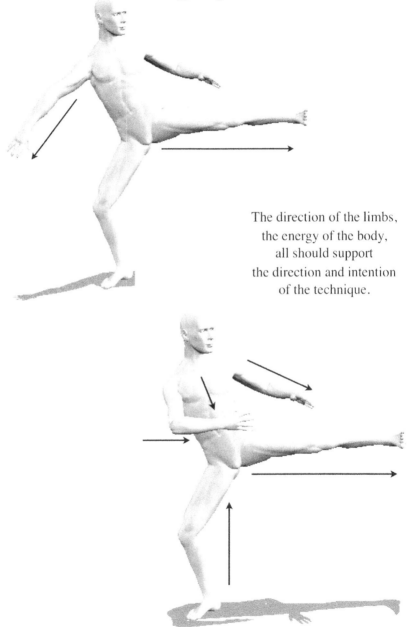

The direction of the limbs,
the energy of the body,
all should support
the direction and intention
of the technique.

CHAPTER SIXTEEN
SPINNING 'POP' KICKS

So I thought I would mention the one side kick that does work, and is a real fight ender.

The problem is that it takes a side kick that works, and then an extra bit of work for the spin and pop.

You don't spin on one leg, you swap legs with a 'pop' spin to the rear.

The leg angles up better, follows the body line so it is harder to see, and it uses the energy of the tan tien.

And there is the problem, the explosive nature of the tan tien is in Karate, and not in kick boxing.

Yet I recommend this kick, especially over the slower and more awkward spinning kick.

CHAPTER SEVENTEEN
SWEEPS

To practice a sweep make sure you don't present the toes. Use the flat of the foot so you don't break any toes.

If sweeps are allowed, you should lift the foot and let them pass.

On the street use the hand to hold the other person's arm, and therefore his body, in place so that you can effect the sweep.

Pull down as you sweep and it will be a double whammy that will make knocking him tot he ground really easy.

I tell you, a person who has to get up from being knocked down is automatically tired. It's sort of like seeing your own blood. It discourages one from fighting.

And, avoid sweeps yourself because you don't want to go to the ground.

You have to learn grappling, and then people might have friends, or maybe you just don't want to roll around on oily, wet, gravely surfaces.

CHAPTER EIGHTEEN
OTHER KICKS

There are lots more kicks. The ax kick, the jumping kick, step spinning kicks, but those tend to be awkward and specialized, and are easy to defend against.

But, that said, I don't not recommend them, I just recommend more work on the basics before you consider these trickier kicks.

The basics are the bread and butter. They are the meat and potatoes. They are the things that work, and the more you delve into the potentials of basics the deeper you dig into your true potential.

Not the ability to fool with a tricky kick, but the ability to make a basic kick work no matter what.

In karate we call this polishing. And it refers to polishing the soul as much as it does polishing a technique.

To polish a basic technique IS to polish the soul.

CHAPTER NINETEEN
BLOCKING

We don't really block, as that is a more karate type term, but we do 'pick off,' or 'cuff' incoming strikes. This is to slap the attacking hand past, or to stick your fist or forearm into the inside path of the incoming punch.

The ideal would be to hit first and fastest.

But sometimes you just have to deal with incoming strikes, and you haven't launched your own, so you pick off the incoming missile.

Very patriotic, that.

There are several things to consider when picking off strikes, and most of them stem from the fact that the other guy is punching because he sees an advantage, which means that you have to deal with a disadvantage.

This brings us to basic kick boxing strategy.

But let's consider blocking kicks briefly before going into strategy.

CHAPTER TWENTY
BLOCKING KICKS

I actually don't believe in blocking kicks. This in spite of the fact that I can do it, and even break a few legs in the accomplishment.

But a kick is aimed for the low part of the body, and it makes no sense to lean forward, or to squat down, to block a kick.

And if the kick is high enough, you are pitting an arm against a leg.

So, if the person kicks low, better to step back. Or, if you are fast enough, strike his leg with an oblique kick. To stomp it.

If the person kicks high, and you can't step away, then block it, work on your blocks until they don't break on the leg, and consider pulling or lifting the kick.

The kick is slow enough, the trick is to watch the body so that you recognize a kick when it is coming, and then move the body enough to get out of the way, and then move the arm with enough harmony to catch the kick and guide it.

Because kicks are slow this is actually doable, but it takes a real amount of work to make it happen.

CHAPTER TWENTY-ONE
BASIC STRATEGY

Imagine yourself standing on a nine square pattern.

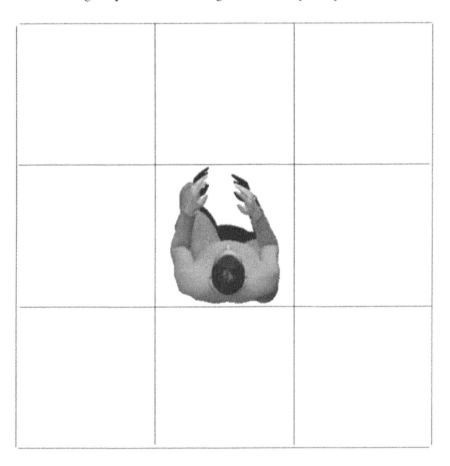

Potentially, attacks can come from any of the eight directions.

If you have the advantage, which is to say it is a poor strike, you don't have to move.

But assuming that a fellow won't attempt a strike unless he perceives an advantage for himself, you will normally have to move, or you will get struck.

For this concept, at this point, let's assume that you are fighting face to face, no attacks from the rear, and no multiple attackers.

If somebody comes from the rear, you turn and re-orient the nine square so you can follow the strategy we are going over here.

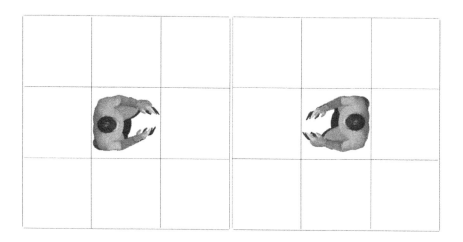

When you face an opponent and the squares share the same front line there is no attack. You haven't stepped on each other's territory, you haven't tried to occupy the same space.

This is the unarmed boundary that countries not at war share.

You can actually feel it when somebody steps on your territory, or you step on theirs. there is a sudden intake of breath, the attack is started, they are in your space, time to do something.

Well, actually, you should have done something before they stepped on your space. You should have angled and shifted so that you would have the advantageous position.

Consider the next illustration.

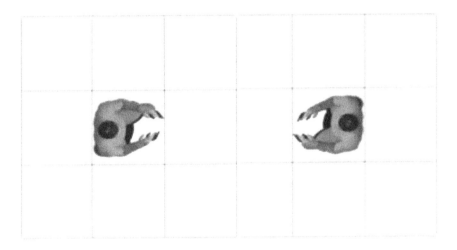

Note that the fourth column of squares to the right is skinny. This is because the fellow on the left moved forward, and his territory is now stepping on the territory of the fellow on the right.

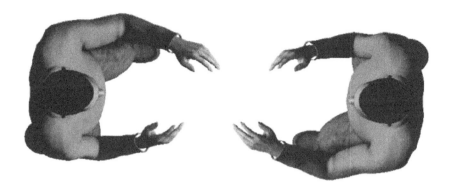

A further close up reveals that the fellows have their arms set in between shoulders and targets.

No matter who punches, an arm is in the way, or close to it.

Now watch what happens in the following pictures as I shift one of the fellows,

The fellow on the right has shifted to his left, and turned slightly to face the fellow on the left. If the fellow on the right attacks with his left hand he will be able to over to override the right hand of the fellow on the left.

In other words, the fellow not he left has shifted towards his forward left square of the nine square pattern he is standing on.

Please be aware that while I am using a nine square, this describes vectors of attack and defense. The actual lines may be circular.

In this illustration the fellow on the right has shifted to his right square, and turned slightly, and now has the advantage of being able to override the left hand of the fellow on the left with his right hand.

Of course, the fellow on the left needs merely turn, and this is merely part of strategy.

And, of course, what if it isn't one hand you're setting up, but the other? This could be a real mind game.

And, we get into the real game of combat: the fellow on the right shifts to the side, the fellow on the left turns, and the fellow on the right shifts back and attacks when the fellow on the left is turning back.

It's all a matter of set up and timing, and that describes the strategy to a tee.

CHAPTER TWENTY-TWO
THE NINE RESPONSES

In this chapter we are going to assume an attack only from the front, from the right front or the left front, and only with the right hand. We are going to go over the possible responses you can make by shifting to any of the eight squares.

Which square you move to will have a different type of response. Here are the eight main responses, but bear in mind that this is a basic overview, and your real response may include other strikes or motions, combining other strikes or motions, etc.

STAY CENTER

If you stay in the same place he's going to hit you, so you must move. We assume he will hit you because he wouldn't have launched a strike without assuming an advantage. And for the sake of this scenario we will assume that he does, in fact, have an advantage.

MOVE FORWARD

You must overpower him, which means striking before he reaches you, or overriding his strike by blasting through with your own.

MOVE FORWARD RIGHT

Override his right hand with your right.

MOVE FORWARD LEFT

Go inside his right hand with your left hand.

MOVE LEFT

Out of range. Kick, or move in, or wait for the left strike and beat it with your right.

MOVE RIGHT

Out of range. Kick, or move in, or wait for the left and beat it with your right.

MOVE LEFT BACK

Out of range. Kick with the right foot.

MOVE RIGHT BACK

Out of range. Kick with the left foot.

MOVE BACK

Out of range. Kick with either foot.

Again, you can, depending on whatever the subtle motions are, duck, choose straight or circular punches or kicks, or do something to play with your opponent's mind.

CHAPTER TWENTY-THREE
MATRIX OF STRIKES

Matrixing is the application of logic to the martial arts. It uses a graph from Boolean algebra. Many people have come across this tool, but none have actually picked it up and run with it. they use it once or twice, don't see the overriding applications for the whole art, and move on.

On the next page is a basic matrix for creating combinations of strikes.

	Jab	Cross	Hook	Upper cut	spin back fist
jab	jab/ jab	jab/ cross	jab/ hook	jab/ u-cut	jab/ spinbf
cross	cross/ jab	cross/ cross	cross/ hook	cross/ u-cut	cross/ spinbf
hook	hook/jab	hook/ cross	hook/ hook	hook/ u-cut	hook/ spinbf
upper cut	u-cut/ jab	u-cut/ cross	u-cut/ hook	u-cut/ u-cut	u-cut/ spinbf
spin back fist	spinbf/ jab	spinbf/ cross	spinbf/ hook	spinbf/ u-cut	spinbf/ spinbf/

Obviously, you can expand this matrix by adding different strikes.

The idea is to be able to do ANY combination.

Many will work easily, some not so easily, and some aren't going to work well at all.

A jab followed by a spin fist is a long way to go. You haven't set yourself up with the jab, so it could be awkward. Or not, depending on how much you practice in exploring these things.

The thing is to make sure you practice enough to make enough the bad ones work.

If something is too difficult to make work, at a certain point you should abandon it.

And the main thing here is that it is sometimes more important to know what doesn't work than what does.

Here's a matrix for kicking.

	front	side	wheel	sweep	spin
front	front front	front side	front wheel	front sweep	front spin
side	side front	side side	side wheel	side sweep	side spin
wheel	wheel front	wheel side	wheel wheel	wheel sweep	wheel spin
sweep	sweep front	sweep side	sweep wheel	sweep sweep	sweep spin
spin	spin front	spin side	spin wheel	spin sweep	spin spin

Again, you can expand this matrix with extra kicks.

You can explore this matrix kicking with one leg, or kicking with two legs in turn.

Some things won't work. A spin followed by a wheel with the same foot is awfully awkward.

But, again, it is just as important, sometimes more important, to know what doesn't work, as well as what does.

Here is a small matrix combining feet and hands.
You can make a bigger matrix as you wish.

	jab	**cross**	**hook**
front	front kick jab	front kick cross	front kick hook
wheel	wheel jab	wheel cross	wheel hook
spinfoot	spinfoot jab	spinfoot cross	spinfoot hook

We are starting the attack with the foot, and following with the hand. This is keeping with the fact that a fight tends to collapse in distance.

You will find an awful lot of awkwardness.

Can you make it some?

And, now that you see the awkwardness, is that going to help you predict what a fighter will follow up a foot attacks with?

Now take the matrix and put the kicks at the top, and the punches down the side.

You are breaking the rule of collapsing distance, but you will learn a lot.

What kicks can you apply inside the hand distance?

When do you have to back up to apply the kick?

And so on.

CHAPTER TWENTY-FOUR
MATRIX OF SQUARES

Speaking of Matrixing, you should improve your footwork, and overall strategies, by drawing a matrix for the concept mentioned in chapter 21.

	1	2	3	4	5	6	7	8	9
1									
2									
3									
4									
5									
6									
7									
8									
9									

The point here is to practice moving from square to square, to find the right footwork to move from square to square, and to select the correct kicks or punches to accompany those moves.

I know it seems like a lot, but if you get a friend and just start exploring by going from 1 - 1 to 1 - 2 and so on to 9 - 9, you will find all sorts of things that work, and that don't work, and you will start understanding these things intuitively.

Intuition is a wonderful thing. People who have it don't have to think, they already know.

A guy in a fight who thinks gets clocked.

A guy who is moving with intuition does the clocking.

Try applying the matrix of punches to the matrix of footwork. See which of the 81 combinations work for which of the nine squares.

CHAPTER TWENTY-FIVE
PASS AND STOP

I know you are probably a bit overwhelmed with all the potentials at this point, so let me make everything a little easier.

Mind you, don't stop going through the matrixes, you need to look at all potentials, but start thinking in binary terms.

You don't have to memorize these matrixes and all the potentials, just go through them and start thinking in terms of binary.

In binary there are only two numbers. Zero and One.

This translates to 'off' and 'on.' Or 'pos' and 'neg.'

Morris code is binary. All you've got is the pedal being clicked, and every letter is defined by the length of the space between clicks. But there is only click, and no click. On and off.

In the martial arts there is a similar concept, though I have never seen anybody say it or represent it.

The binary concepts in the martial arts are 'pass' and 'stop.'

When a punch comes you either let it go (miss), or you stop it with a block of some sort.

This is a very simple thing based on body positioning.

We can get tremendously complex with the various systems and their ideas of what effective blocks are, but kick boxing becomes quite pure, especially since there are not regimented block but only slaps to guide a punch past, or sticking your glove in the way and 'picking off' the punch.

And, you are either punching or not.

And a punch is an object that flows (has trajectory), and the only two consequences are a miss (exhausting), or a hit.

Very binary, kick boxing.

CHAPTER TWENTY-SIX
FIGHTING STRATEGY

Having made Kicking Boxing easy with the binary concept, let's discuss fighting strategy.

The weapons you have in the martial arts are weapons, kicking, punching, kneeing, elbowing, takedowns (grappling).

The complete matrix on this is in the Matrix Kung Fu course at Monster Martial Arts, and I recommend it. After all, the street does not limit itself to kicks and punches.

But, since we are staying within the confines of a specific sport, you have two weapons. These are the kick and the punch. Here is the matrix.

	kick	punch
kick	kick/kick	kick/punch
punch	punch/kick	punch/punch

Thus, you have four potential basic combinations.

Kick and kick again.

Kick and punch.

Punch and kick.

Punch and punch again.

If you wish to go to three strikes (or more) in a combination, it is easy enough to visualize.

Kick/kick/kick

Kick/kick/punch

Kick/punch/punch

Kick/punch/kick

Punch/punch/punch

Punch/punch/kick

Punch/kick/kick

Punch/kick/punch

Thus, there are only four two strike combinations, and there are only eight three strike combinations.

Twelve 'techniques' is easy enough to work on.

Further, you could split the techniques and have a beginner work on just the four, and a more advanced student work on the eight.

The difficulty comes in when you designate what a specific kick is, or a punch. Then we end up with a matrix so large as to be unwieldy.

Although, I do recommend that you get a big poster board and make a big matrix.

Across the top of the matrix you can list: jab/cross/hook/uppercut/spin fist/front kick/side kick/wheel kick/ spin kick, and so on.

Down the side you can list: jab/cross/hook/uppercut/spin fist/front kick/side kick/wheel kick/ spin kick, and so on.

And you can mix this matrix up by applying a matrix of the possible sides of the body.

	right side	left side
right side	right/right	right/left
left side	left/right	left/left

So let's look at one of these potentials.

The first thing is going to be a jab/jab. This uses the front hand, and will work on right/right, and left/left, but not on right/left and left/right, unless you change your footwork, which is not heavily recommended in a fight.

And, the second item is going to be jab/cross. This will work with right/left and left/right, but not on right/right and left/left, unless you change your feet.

Okay, you can see where this is going.

Let's look at an uppercut/spin kick. This is going to be awkward, because you have to translate the direction of the power, forward and up, to a spin laterally with the hips, while close in. Yikes and ugh!

You can make it work, and it is worthwhile taking apart the techniques (combinations) that don't work, and seeing what you have to do to make it work. At the least this will prepare you for those awkward times when you are out of position for whatever reason.

So you execute an uppercut, what change of body position (what square in the nine square must you step to), to make this work?

If it's a right uppercut, depending on the impact, you might fall back to the left rear square. Or, maybe the opponent will step backwards so that you are in the left rear square. Maybe.

There are so many things that could happen, so many potentials of motion, of hits and misses, that the conjecturing could take a while, and be pretty in depth.

But think about it. think about it for every combination on the matrix, and for every combination of body side (right/left) you present, or get stuck with.

The real point here is that no matter what is happening in a fight, there is a potential way to turn ANY situation to your advantage. The real question is have you gone through the potentials sufficient that your mind becomes intuitive as to your possible responses.

CHAPTER TWENTY-SEVEN
THE ALLEY

With all the potentials of the last chapter it is advisable to inject a simplifying concept. In this case, the concept is the Alley.

I will go into The Alley properly in just a moment, but before you do The Alley you have to establish the proper distance. I refer to this establishment of distance as 'The Line.'

Advance, close with your opponent, step on The Line and observe his reaction. The reaction may be subtle (a slight widening of the eyes, etc.) or it may be gross (he jumps back).

Before this reaction you are in kicking range, or too far away for anything.

Once you step on this 'line,' once you encroach in his territory, you are in punching distance.

I have written about this in other places, specifically 'Bruce Lee vs Classical Martial Arts,' available on Amazon, so let me just move from the distance into The Alley.

Once you are moving into punching distance spread your hands slightly and leave an 'alley' for your opponent to punch through.

If you open the hands you leave him a path, and he will become predictable. If you close your hands he will have to go around, which, again, makes him predictable.

So in kickboxing you control 'The Line,' and make it predictable whether he punches or kicks.

Then you control The Alley, and make the punch predictable.

This is an excellent and simple way to control strategies.

And, obviously, you can shade or tilt the alley, or whatever, and even control which hand he punches with, and what he punches with.

I tell you this strategy, and advise you that it is a martial arts strategy.

It can still be effective in the ring, however.

The reason it isn't is because people train for the technique, for speed and muscle and all that, and not for awareness.

Practicing these tricks, making them into drills, will make you aware, and I tell you this: all things being equal, it is the fighter with the most awareness that will win.

And…even if things are unequal, awareness gives an edge of unbelievable magnitude.

The fight doesn't always go to the strong, especially not if you become versed in these tactics.

CHAPTER TWENTY-EIGHT
THE CLINCH

A clinch happens for one simple reason: a fight tends to collapse in distance.

It has to collapse in distance, because you have to close to strike, and thus the tendency is to always move forward, and little attention is given to the retreat.

And even if there is a retreat, the fighter who is causing the retreat (winning) will advance, and even faster.

So, what is the solution when you have been out advanced, can't retreat, are overwhelmed?

Clinch.

And, there is one simple strategy that you must follow in a clinch. And you should follow this strategy when you are in a corner, up against the ropes, or whatever.

Relax. Sag on the opponent. Let him use up his muscles supporting you. Don't use your muscles, don't contest, don't keep bulling.

And don't let yourself get bullied.

Relax. Let him get tired of supporting you, and wait for the ref to break you apart.

This strategy has obvious weaknesses in a street fight, and in that case you are advised to use whatever muscle, and to learn the fine points of tripping, grappling, elbowing, head butting, and so on.

This is, in fact, one of the places where you want to practice an art that doesn't bind the hands with gloves, and practices nasty, little tricks like eye gouging, kneeing the groin, and so on.

CHAPTER TWENTY-NINE
THE TACTIC OF POSITIONING

You want to present your opponent with a wedge, your body wedged so that he has few targets, but must deal with all your weapons.

And, you want to work him so that he is 'flat' to you, not wedged, but open, giving you lots of targets and not having his weapons in the way.

Simply, draw a line between his feet, and move around so that you can cross the line with your wedge.

I mentioned the Bruce Lee book, and I advise you look to Bruce Lee's art, whether through my books or not, because that art is highly developed. It is especially developed for the street, for a real fight, and it is like kick boxing on steroids. The drills and concepts are simply top notch, and are easily adapted to the ring.

CHAPTER THIRTY
THE MIRROR DRILL EXPANDED

It's time for me to give you a simple solo drill.

The drill is to shadow box in a mirror. Study yourself. Close up openings, learn how to be suble in presenting The Alley, perfect your kicks, and so on.

Most people know of the Mirror Drill, so let's take it a bit further.

Get a partner, stand twenty feet apart, and fight slowly.

Watch each other, one shifts, the other responds.

One sets up The Alley. The other enters or not. And you watch what happens.

One kicks (is blocked) and punches (takes it on the jaw and spin fists)

And so on.

You are not one foot apart banging. You are not 20 feet apart banging.

You are 20 feet apart and moving in slow motion, getting the long view, and a microscopic view, of how you are moving, of how the other guy moves, and so on.

This is actually quite fun, and you are going to find you and your partner getting a little goofy. After all, you can try stupid stuff, you can pretend you're in the movies, you can play…but what you are really doing is increasing your awareness. Learning, but with a microscope.

One would not think that being at telescopic distance would result in microscopic learning, but it really does.

CHAPTER THIRTY-ONE
THE TYPES OF FIGHTERS

There are several types of fighters. Interestingly, there have been many versions, or perhaps I should say attempts, to classify fighters. One book classified the types of fighters like this:

The Hit and Runner ~ basically, a sniper. Doesn't want to close and get hit, just wants to do the hit with no risk.

The Overwhelmer ~ bigger than you, at least in his mind, he closes and just keeps punching.

The Counter Puncher ~ Waiting for you to make a mistake.

The Long Range Fighter ~ Trusts his kicks, doesn't want to get hit.

The Cross Stance Fighter ~ You have your right foot forward, he has his left foot forward.

This is an interesting classification.

The Hit and Runner can be confused with a Counter Puncher, and the Cross Stance fighter should be in a matrix.

To unconfuse this specific concept of a 'cross fighter' let me offer a Matrix.

	right side forward	left side forward
right side forward	right to right	right to left
left side forward	left to right	left to left

You can express this binarily: Same side forward or cross side forward.

Other people have offered other classifications for the types of fighters, but the best one I came across was presented by Joe Lewis, but which may have been originated by Bruce Lee, or was modified from Bruce Lee's theories.

The three types of fighters, and this is particularly specific to Kick Boxing, are: Runner, Blocker, Charger.

A runner is going to dance away, keep distance, he will be a counter puncher or a sniper.

A blocker is going to stand his ground, deal with what comes, and is willing to trade blows.

A charger goes forward, attempting to overwhelm with brute power/speed.

I like this classification because it is very Neutronic. Neutronics is the study of the human being doing the fighting, that which is aware in a fighter, and can be studied at Churchof MartialArts.com.

Neutronic theory holds that the universe is filled with objects that have trajectory (flow). Thus, an object is either going towards you, away from you, or holding distance. This is useful for analyzing the motion of bodies, and of fists, and is easily adapted to various strategies.

So here is a matrix for the three types of fighters.

	blocker	runner	charger
blocker	block/block	block/run	block/charge
runner	run/block	run/run	run/charge
charger	charge/block	charge/run	charge/charge

If you subscribe to a different method of classifying the types, make a matrix for those types.

But using the matrix I have provided, there are several ways to use it.

The first word describes one person, and the second word describes the second person.

So the first square would have a blocker fighting a blocker. They would spar, contain the distance, bide their time, and look for the opening.

The second box, block/run, would have a blocker fight a runner. This doesn't make sense. If the guy is running, what is there to block?

The third box, block/charge. One is charging and the other is blocking. Might be moving backwards slowly, but is not running.

The fourth box, run/block. Same as the second box. Distance, and the fight, is not collapsing, so it is hard to figure, and there's not much threat, and so on. Eventually, the runner will turn the blocker into a charger, but no guarantees.

The fifth box, run/run. Might as well shake hands and talk.

The sixth box, run/charge. A perfectly matched pair. The fight will go to the person who is better at his specific strategy.

The seventh box, charge/block. Same as the third box.

The eighth box, charge run. Same as the sixth box.

The ninth box, charge/charge. Zingo bingo, we gots a fight! These guys are the stuff of marketing dreams. One will end up unconscious, and the other more unconscious. But who cares so long as the box office does a landslide business, eh?

Now, three of the boxes are repeats, and the basic concepts are this:

Runner and Blockers and the fight might not be all that much. After all, the runner and the blocker aren't aggressively going for the knock out.

So a fight has to have people who move forward (Chargers), or at least hold their space (Blockers) against Chargers, and that leaves only a certain number of boxes as realistic strategies between types of fighters.

That all said, the point here is that you have to know what kind of fighter you are fighting, and this is ALWAYS easily ascertainable.

Simply move forward and step on 'The Line.'

The Runner moves back instinctively.

The Blocker holds his ground, adjusts his hands, gets ready.

The Charger and you suddenly have a flurry of strikes in your face.

So it is easy to figure out what type of fighter you are fighting, and then you have to figure out what kind of fighter you want to be in response.

So you step on 'The Line,' you watch, and you analyze his size and speed and strength and which foot is forward and how he holds his hands and so on, then you choose the type of fighter you think is going to be able to beat him.

And, to be specific, let me go over the factors I analyze when I step into the ring with somebody.

First, I analyze his body. Is he thick? Tall? Muscular? Whippy? What?

Second I analyze the way he holds his body. Does he stand like a wrestler? Flat footed and ready to take you down? Does he bounce like he wants to jab?

Third, I analyze his stance. Is he bouncing so that he can move in any direction? Is he standing and less mobile?

Fourth, which side is forward? Which side am I going to have to deal with. Is he same side or cross side? Is he easily manipulated to change sides? to a particular side?

Fifth, is he standing so he can use his feet? Does he look like he prefers feet? Which foot? What kick?

Sixth, how is he holding his hands? How will The Alley work on him?

Seventh, straight puncher or circular?

Eight, is he a Clincher? Does he look like a bully? Can I waste him by clinching?

Now, there are lots of other things that will come to mind as you go down this checklist. But going down these items, before you even close with him, is going to tell you an immense amount, and might even save your bacon.

And, if it isn't accurate, if you misjudge, then adjusting after the fact is very easy, because you can re-evaluate by this checklist, or just go to the Blocker/Runner/Charger matrix.

CHAPTER THIRTY-TWO
THE MATRIX

I just want to emphasize a point here.

A matrix is a tool. It is only as good or as bad as you understand it, as you use it.

The point of a matrix is not just to strategize, though I am sure you have come to a conclusion as to that benefit, but to acquaint you with ALL potentials of motion.

What beats a fellow is not lack conditioning, or skills, so much as what he doesn't know.

When the guy does something you don't understand, then you get beat.

And when you are in a position where you don't know what to do, you get beat.

But matrixing uncovers ALL the potentials of motion, and so there shouldn't be anything he can do that you haven't seen, and visualized, and even worked on from both the viewpoint of attacker and defender. This is the real value of Matrixing: the expansion of your awareness so that there is nothing you don't understand, nothing that fools you.

CHAPTER THIRTY-THREE
CHANGING TYPES OF FIGHTERS

If a person is a Charger, and you are Charger, you better hope you have better conditioning.

If a person is a Charger and you are a blocker, you better hope your blocks are strong enough to deal with the bull.

If a person is a Charger and you are a Runner, you better hope you can run better than he can charge.

The real key here is to hit without getting hit. This is actually a Matrixing datum, or formula.

The purpose of a fight is to avoid getting struck, while delivering your own strike.

So you sidestep, keep circling, let him waste himself and pick him off.

If a person is a Blocker and you are a Charger, you are going to have to ride right over his strikes, absorb punishment, and give him more punishment.

If a person is Blocker and you are a Blocker, you are in for a chess match. The game will go to the person who is slicker and trickier.

If a person is a Blocker and you are a Runner, you are going to have a rough time. He's too smart to follow you, and you are eventually going to have to change your game, and you are changing into a game he has been playing for a while.

It is not bad to be a Runner. A lot of fights have been avoided by running.

But, when you have to fight, it is better not to run, but to get the job done. This is especially true for the street.

This is backed up by the fact of the martial arts themselves, most techniques are based on aggressive action, and almost never on backing up.

This is true even, and sometimes especially, of such arts as Tai Chi Chuan and Aikido.

If you are a runner I suggest you move forward in your martial arts training and learn how to go forward. Even if it is not what you prefer, you have to learn how to do this. Until you do this you will almost always be at a disadvantage.

In chess, in the event of a perfect game, white will win, simply for that fact that white makes the first move.

If a person is a Runner, and you are a Charger, have fun.

If a person is a Runner, and you are a Blocker, be patient. Make him change his game.

If a person is a Runner, and you are a Runner, shake hands and give each other a big hug.

CHAPTER THIRTY-FOUR
ANALYSIS OF FIGHTERS

I want to go through some of the things you are going to have to think about if you are a Kick Boxer. This is going to be a little loose in structure, but that's the way a fight is sometimes, and it will go beyond the bounds of the checklist I offered earlier.

What kind of guard does he have? Some people like the half guard, with the front arm down and the rear hand guarding the face, but that front arm is pretty important weapon to have half out of action before the fight even starts. It smacks of a person who hasn't trained enough, and is resting his front arm.

Speaking of resting, whenever you are at a distance you can drop the arms, but don't have those arms down when the distance closes.

Is he wasting energy with uneconomical movements? Bouncing is fine, but too much is just a waste. Not enough and you'll let the opponent settle down too much. Use the bouncing to keep him off balance, don't give him space to relax.

What is wrong with this picture?

The stance is too wide. This fellow can get kicked in the groin (on the street), or have an inside sweep done to him.

When he punches, does he drop one or both of the arms? How can you take advantage of that?

What is wrong with this picture?

This fellow has his elbows too far out. It doesn't look like much, but it opens his belly. Keep the elbows tight to discourage body shots.

However, if you are at distance, possibly you can sucker a kick in, and drop those elbows down on his instep.

Speaking of sweeps, make sure you don't sweep with pointed toes. You'll break them. Turn the foot so you can sweep with the sole.

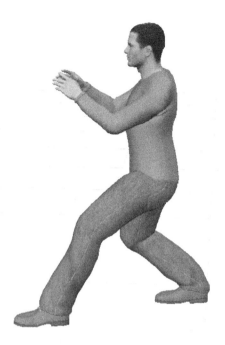

What's wrong with this picture?

He is in a classical karate stance. This is a great stance for karate, but not for kick boxing. It cements him in place and limits his weapons. It is, however, great if you don't want to bounce, but want to work on the 'waiting game' of the gunfighter.

Does fatigue make your opponent drop his arms? Is there anything else that happens because of fatigue?

What's wrong with this picture?

The arms are too high. He's protecting his face at the cost of his body.

BTW, his hands can actually obscure his vision in this position.

Does he have a pattern of attack that is too regular? Make a list of possibilities and ways to exploit these possibilities.

What's wrong with this picture?

His arms have spread to the sides. This indicates poor balance. Can you name a few ways to take advantage of this?

What weapon does he lead with the most?

Does he use feints? A fake is a wasted motion, can you spot them and hit him between he fake and the real punch?

What's wrong with this picture?

Leaning too far forward. You need to be balanced between forward and back, side to side. Not too high, not too low.
You need to find the proper balance for everything.

Does he telegraph what he is doing? How? How can you take advantage of this?

Does he learn from his mistakes? Or does he keep on bashing with the same old same old regardless of what it costs him?

Do you learn from your mistakes?

Remember, a mistake is an opportunity to learn.

Is his timing or distance off?

Is a meat and potatoes man? Or does he try flashy or unworkable techniques?

Does he fight on a wing and a prayer? Or has he done his homework on you?

Does he use the ring? Or is he tied to a single angle of attack, mode of attack?

Which type of fighter is he?

Does he have enough power to knock somebody out?

Can he endure? Can he take a punch and keep coming back?

Do you change what you are doing? Are you tricky and deceptive? Can others figure you out easily?

CHAPTER THIRTY-FIVE
TIMING

I know some people say timing doesn't matter.

Oh, those deluded fools.

That just shows they have NO understanding of kick boxing, or any other art or sport.

A fight is ALL timing. As soon as your sense of time dwindles you are going to get hit, and your punches are going to miss.

You need timing to throw combination. You have to see the response, and then have sufficient timing to go through the open door you've just created.

You need timing with your footwork. You need to time the arms with the legs just right, or you're going to walk into something.

And you need to time the opponent's punches and kicks. You need to see when they are going to happen, and adjust your own sense of time accordingly.

Here's a timing trick.

Bounce with him, just one or two bounces, don't do it too long or he'll pick up on you. Then speed up and sweep.

The point of timing is this: Timing establishes an awareness of when the universe moves so you can best take advantage of this motion.

CHAPTER THIRTY-SIX
WHAT TIME IS

The interesting thing is that nobody really understands what time is. I say this after asking people for several decades, and ALWAYS getting the incorrect answer.

I ask them what 'time' is, because if they don't understand time then how can they have timing?

They say: when the universe goes past.

And this is the best answer I get. Most people don't even come this close.

Time is a measurement of distance.

The length 'time' it takes for a runner to go from point A to point B. That's time.

Time is how we estimate the passage (in real terms) of the universe.

Time is how long it takes for his fist to reach your jaw, and vice versa.

And all this brings us to an interesting point.

You have heard me talk about awareness, and now time, and the two coincide delightfully.

You see, you need awareness to appreciate time.

So let's say you enter the ring with Bad Jo Jo on a dare. He outweighs you, he's got more muscles than King Kong, and he's even in shape.

He clocks you. An interesting word, 'clock,' now that we are talking about time.

And you are half unconscious. No longer aware, and now you can't estimate the TIME it takes for his fist to reach your face.

Hmm.

Here's another bad one.

You sit on the sidelines drinking your brewski and cheering, and your man, the guy you bet on, is getting his face pummeled. And every punch he throws is a MISS.

You scream, you rant, but it's too late.

He has accumulated so much punishment, and your boy is a dog.

What happened? He got punched in the face, which rattled his brain a bit, and his perceptions are off, and he can no longer hit that part of the universe represented by his opponent's face.

But it gets worse.

Let's talk about this last scenario a bit.

When you punch, and miss his face, it is because you are punching where he was, and not where he will be. So you no longer know where the universe is…you can only go where you think it is, where it used to be.

And now we come to the worst of all. Or, the best, if you are following what I have saying and are ready to learn something very, very important.

In offering the preceding scenarios, in discussing lost of timing due to trauma, we come to an interesting little fact:

reaction time

Let me make this really quick and simple.

The part of the word 're-' means after. So you are moving 'after' the action.

That means you are always behind what is happening, you are not making things happening. You are responding, and are not the cause.

Training your reaction time is therefore self-defeating. And punching and missing because you have been 'clocked' (there's that word again) is doubly defeating.

The point here is that you shouldn't be training reaction time, you should be training in intuition.

You should be learning to fight not because something happened, but because you know what is happening…and will happen.

So here is your problem, in a sport aimed at improving reaction time, how are you going to learn and adapt to intuition?

Interesting choice you've got.

CHAPTER THIRTY-SEVEN
MORE DRILLS

Some of what I present here I have stated in Blinding Steel, a course available at <u>MonsterMartialArts.com</u>, and I have described it in other places.

Start by creating drills out of the combinations presented in the Matrixes in chapter 22..

You can obviously do these drills with focus pads, but I prefer, whenever possible, to use a body shield. The reason is that with a body shield you have to move a whole body weight with every strike. If you don't move the body with a strike, it is weak, and you need to practice.

For a jab/jab, pick off each jab with the same hand.

And, if you want to include the matrixing of right to left, then pick off the jabs with one hand and then the other.

For jab/hook (to the body), pick off the jab, and absorb the hook with the bag.

And so on.

And this brings us to the drill I prefer and teach. I do this mostly for Karate or Kung Fu classes, but you can adapt it to kick boxing as you wish.

Label the limbs as follows:

Right leg is number one.

Left leg is number two.

Right arm is number three.

Left arm is number four

Spinning is number five.

Call out a sequence of numbers, and have the kick boxer attack in that sequence.

Let's say you call 1 - 3.

He must kick with the right leg and then punch with the right hand.

I usually start with two strike combinations, and get the student very comfortable, usually a couple of weeks or a month, and then go to three strike combinations.

Let's say I called 2 - 3 - 5.

The kick boxer should respond with a left kick, a right punch, and then spin in place with a kick or punch.

The kick boxer is going to have to develop a sense of distance to choose the right weapon, foot or fist, for the spin.

The person holding the kicking shield should be forced back with every strike.

With very advanced kick boxers you can have the shield holder vary distance very slightly. But this is very advanced, and you should drill the kick boxer MUCH before allowing this.

CHAPTER THIRTY-EIGHT
CONTROLLING A FIGHT

It is true that you have to be able to change. Here is a matrix of the basic changes.

	enter	close	finish
enter	enter/enter	enter/close	enter/finish
close	close/enter	close/close	close/finish
finish	finish/enter	finish/close	finish/finish

I use these terms on matrixing courses available at MonsterMartialArts. They originally referred to such things as initiating the action (with a kick or punch), closing the distance (with a knee or elbow), and finishing the fight (takedown or knock out).

Here, kick boxing being rather limited in weapons, they refer to the initiation of action, the closure of distance, and the knock out.

So the first box, enter/enter. Two fellows jabbing, but never closing or offering combination.

The second box, enter/close. A strike (kick) and a closure of distance to another strike (punch).

The third box, enter/finish. A kick or punch from a distance that succeeds in knock out.

The fourth box, close/enter. Closing to a punch, then changing the mind and backing out. Maybe the set up wasn't good enough, or maybe the other guy mounted a good defense that made further action inadvisable.

The fifth box, close/close. Both fighters move forward and exchange punches. If there is not finesse, then the fellow who is better at punching is going to win.

The sixth box, close/finish. A punch and a knock out.

The seventh, eighth, and ninth boxes. You finish him off before you enter or close the fight. Nice trick if you can do it.

CHAPTER THIRTY-NINE
THE OVERVIEW

We are coming to a conclusion here, and I just want to mention a few points one should consider as a kick boxer.

Make a plan. Don't go in blind and trust that your muscle is enough. Make a plan for your life, for your work outs, and for each and every combat you enter into.

Find your opponent's weaknesses. Don't just bull in and trust that you will learn 'on the fly.' If the other guy has a plan and you don't, you're going to be lying down and he won't.

Cancel out your opponent's strengths. Be accurate in assessing what you are going up against, and figure out precise methods for handling your opponent's strong points.

Take control. Don't start fighting after your opponent, or because of something he does. Take control and establish how the fight will be fought, or even if there will be aright in the first place.

Control the distance. Control how close you are, close the distance when you want to. Control of the distance is one of the most crucial points of any fight. It establishes choice of weapons, strategy, and so many other things.

Reverse a losing situation. Man, if you are taking it on the chin, do something different. Change your plan. Make a plan specifically for situations in which he is better than you. Lok to your matrixes to find out potential losing situations where he might be better at something than you.

Mess up his timing. Never let him get set. Whenever he thinks he's got you figured out, change up and shift and alter what you do.

Choose the range. Decide what you are best at, and what he is worst at, and fight at that distance. Be adept at all distances, but analyze the other fighter so you can be the best while he is at his worst.

Polish your technique. Never stop thinking that you can't be better. That extra millisecond of timing, that extra millimeter of thrust, those are crucial to exploit if you want to be a winner.

Choose what type of fighter you are going to be. Make him be the type of fighter you want to face. Figure out how to make people alter their strategies, and what types of fighters they would prefer to be. Make them move into weakness and away from strength, while you move into strength and away from weakness.

There are three elements to a fighter: speed, strength, and technique. Work on all three, but know that technique is the most important. When the other fighter has an edge in speed and strength, technique can always win you the day.

Condition yourself to go 15 rounds. Yes, kick boxing frequently only has three rounds. But hit the road, do the bike or the skip rope, and train yourself NEVER to run out of gas.

Train yourself to take a punch. Have people drop medicine balls on your belly. Have people hit you slowly and methodically, figure out what exercises you need to do to tighten up various targets on the body.

Train at a study rate. Dont' try to get it all done in one day, rather improve the body, the limbs, as a unit. Don't forget the ligaments and work on the muscles only. Don't train in bursts, train for the long hail with occasional bursts.

Train for accuracy. One punch to the face is always better than ten punches that miss.

Analyze and visualize. Do your homework, and imagine yourself winning the fight. Get VERY detailed in seeing exactly how you will win. If you visualize, it will happen.

Trust what you know.

Do not use emotion; use intention. Intention bred by determination and persistence. Emotion actually stops you from analyzing, and will lead you to mistakes and errors in judgement.

Learn to stay focused. Especially late in the fight, especially when your muscles are screaming and the pain is starting: that is when you need to keep your mind apart from the confusion and hurt.

Hold to the plan until you can't, but as soon as the game plan isn't working, recognize that moment and change.

See your goal. Dont' just think about it, or fantasize, SEE IT! Visualize so strongly that it becomes as real a a punch to the gut.

Decide what you want, then get it, and don't let anything stop you from getting it…especially yourself. Remember, there is no man that is not self made, so make yourself the way you want to be, and don't take no for an answer.

CHAPTER FORTY
CONCLUSION

Kick boxing is a great sport.

I encourage you to train hard, but to train smart.

Don't be dismissive of other sports or arts. There is much to be learned, much that can improve your sport, in such as Karate, Aikido, or whatever. Just as they can learn from you.

In Karate belts are offered as goals. A black belt takes about four years, and there are other belts to measure the smaller steps.

So what 'belt' do you want to be in a month? Do you want to master the basics? Do you want a certain level of conditioning?

Where do you want to be in a year? What level of fighter do you want to be?

What about three years?

What about when you are 65?

Don't get unreal and just say 'I want to be the best, man!'

Figure out how many push ups you want to be able to do, how many miles you want to be able to run, how many rounds you want to be able to survive.

Write these goals down, put them where you can see them, and drive yourself towards them.

About the Author

Al Case walked into his first martial arts school in 1967. During the Gold Age of Martial Arts he studied such arts as Aikido, Wing Chun, Ton Toi Northern Shaolin, Fut Ga Southern Shaolin, Weapons, Tai Chi Chuan, Pa Kua Chang, and others.

In 1981 he began writing for the martial arts magazines, including Inside Karate, Inside Kung Fu, Black Belt, Masters and Styles, and more.

In 1991 he was asked to write his own column in Inside Karate.

Beginning in 2001 he completed the basic studies of Matrixing, a logic approach to the Martial Arts he had been working on for over 30 years.

2011 he was heavily immersed in creating Neutronics, the science behind the science of Matrixing.

Interested martial artists can avail themselves of his research into Matrixing and Neutronics at MonsterMartialArts.com.

Continue the Journey!

If you are looking for other martial arts to compliment your education, on the next few pages you can find books and courses to aid you.

I specifically recommend Matrix Karate. Matrix Karate has the 'Matrix of Blocks,' which can be applied to the techniques you have seen in this volume, and which can expand your repertoire of usable techniques into hundreds of combat ready tricks.

If you are more interested in grappling, I recommend Matrix Kung Fu, which has the complete list of stand up takedowns.

For a complete list of Martial Arts video instruction courses, go to:

MonsterMartialArts.com

THE 'HOW TO CREATE KENPO KARATE' SERIES!

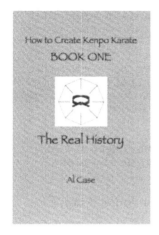

The most incredible analysis of Kenpo Karate in the world.
In depth Matrixing of over 150 Kenpo techniques.
New ways of doing Kenpo forms.
New ways of teaching and structuring classes.
A COMPLETE REWORK OF ONE OF THE MOST
IMPORTANT MARTIAL ARTS SYSTEMS IN THE WORLD!
Over 40,000 words
Nearly 400 pages
Over 800 graphics
Only possible through…

the logic of Matrixing!

The History of Matrixing

Matrixing is the cumulation of decades of research. Among the dozens of martial arts studied, Al Case kept specific records of five up to the point of Matrixing breakthroughs. The following five books are the encyclopedia of the history of matrixing.

These books are not arcane histories, but records of forms learned, techniques mastered, drills done, and so on. They provide, in addition, a linkage from Chinese martial arts through Karate to Matrix Karate, which was the first Matrixing course.

Pan Gai Noon (half hard/half soft) is a style of Chinese Kung Fu originally taught about 1900.

It was taught by a street hawker named Shu Shi Wa, and may have had roots in the Temple Gung Fu of the times.

It eventually was transformed into a style of Karate called Uechi Ryu.

The style therefore links Karate to Kung Fu, which makes it one of the more important martial arts, historically and technically speaking.

In this volume the art of Pan Gai Noon has been resurrected through the logic of Matrixing.

The first two forms, plus drills and techniques, are presented, making this a valuable addition to any martial artist's library.

Available on Amazon

Kang Duk Won Korean Karate, the one Karate that resulted in the development of the five Korean systems which later became Taekwondo.

This is a pure form of Karate from before the Funakoshi and Japanese influence.

It was chosen by the Imperial bodyguards of three different nations, Okinawa, Korea, and Japan.

Available on Amazon

Kwon Bup is a form of American Karate developed by Sensei Robert Babich of the Kang Duk Won. It is linear and powerful, and the ultimate expression of the only American to ever do the 'One Finger Trick.'

Sensei Babich could thrust a finger through a board and not break it, but leave a hole. This is his art, his forms and techniques, his method of bringing Karate to the highest stage.

Available on Amazon

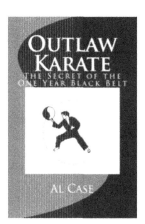

Outlaw Karate is the synthesis of two methods of Karate, Kang Duk Won (House for Espousing Virtue), and Kwon Bup (The Fist Method).

    These arts were stripped of duplicate movements and poser techniques, then boiled down to six easy to learn (and thus easy to use) forms.

    The result was a form of Karate that could be taught in less than one year, while keeping the original power of Karate, and even enhancing it.

    This art set the stage for breakthroughs in the Martial Science of Matrixing. *Available on Amazon*

Any karate student wishing to learn an extremely powerful form of Karate, and to delve into the history of Matrixing, should definitely look into Outlaw Karate.

Available on Amazon

Buddha Crane Karate.

Matrixing is a form of logic.

While it can be used in any endeavor, it is specific to the Martial Arts.

Buddha Crane Karate is a very pivotal Martial Art as it was created just as the author was figuring out the logic of Matrixing.

In this book you get to see the exact thought process that is Matrixing at work; you will see the principles which would later crop up in his courses on Matrixing.

In addition, Buddha Crane is an entire Martial Art, built from the ground up. Thus you get to see exactly, how and why an art takes form. This will definitely enlighten any who wish to inspect their own martial art and truly understand what they are seeing.

Available on Amazon

Stand Alone Martial Arts Books

Following are stand alone books on a variety of martial arts. Matrixing has been used extensively to make these arts quicker, faster, and easier to understand.

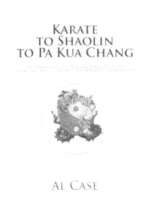

Karate to Shaolin to Pa Kua Chang

The book that traces the evolution of internal power from Karate to Gung Fu.

There are three manuals in this volume, and they are designed to take the martial arts student from the hard knuckles of karate to the soft, internal practices of Gung Fu.

This book contains forms, techniques, training drills, and the theory necessary to help a student evolve quickly and natural.

Available on Amazon

Matrixing Tongbei

Introduces Tong Bei (through the back) Gung Fu. This includes basic theory and drills for creating a certain 'emptiness' inside the body.

Includes many matrixes for full and complete understanding of Tong Bei techniques.

This book is actually an introduction to the 'MonkeyBoxing' taught by Al Case. The complete line up of Monkey Boxing courses starts with this book, 'Matrixing Tong Bei,' and continues with the video instruction courses 'Blinding Steel,' and 'Matrixing Kung Fu (Monkey Boxing).

Available on Amazon

Fixing MCMAP: How to Make the Marine Corps Martial Arts into a True Martial Art

Military organizations the world over have long practiced martial arts, so the Marines decided they should have the best fighting art in the world. MCMAP is the result of intense research. A research conducted in the arena of real life and death struggles.

MCMAP is good. Really good, but there are some weaknesses in the system. There were certain limits on it, such as top level fighting was reserved only for men who advanced in rank. And, there were weaknesses such as no kicking structure, the system was designed with boxing as the template, weapons fighting was not taught as one, efficient subject, and so on.

FIXING MCMAP fixes these problems. So the person who studies these two volumes, Fixing MCMAP volume 1 and 2, will not only get the whole Marine Corps fighting system, but they will get the improved and fixed system. A system with no errors, and designed to make a true art, and which will make the BEST FIGHTING MEN IN THE WORLD!

Available on Amazon

Bruce Lee vs Classical Martial Arts

The most advanced book on Jeet Kune Do ever written. This book uses Matrixing, and even Neutronics, to finally and fully and completely understand The Little Dragon. Is Jeet Kune Do truly the best martial art in the world? When you apply Matrixing to it it may well be.

Yogata (The Yoga Kata)

The oldest exercise system in the world is at last put to a scientifically designed form. Easy to do, yet covers ALL the basics of Yoga. Good for warm up, cool down, or rehabilitating injuries.

This one form will enhance your martial arts, and your life, far beyond just doing the martial arts.

Black Belt Yoga

The art of Yoga arranged scientifically. Makes for MUCH faster progress in Yoga.

Instead of nibbling away at postures one at a time, the student discovers the totality of the method, and can see the end of the tunnel.

Why this hasn't been done before is actually one of the great mysteries of the world. It just makes SO-O-O much sense.

Matrixing Gung Fu!

The Shaolin Butterfly

The training manual from the original Shaolin Butterfly Course. Specific attention to matrixing footwork. A great book for those who wish to step off the linear footwork of Karate.

Of special interest is the transition from Shaolin to Pa Kua Chang. This is the first time this secret has ever been revealed.

Butterfly Pa Kua Chang

The training manual from the original Butterfly Pa Kua Chang course.

Completely demystifies the art. Things that were mystical are now totally explained in English and excellent physics.

The Hardest Punch in the World

A virtual doctoral thesis on how to have the most powerful punch in the world. A breakdown of the types of punches, and the training sequence that must be followed. To not follow the sequence is to miss out on the real power. Includes such things as the paper punch, the water punch, the fire punch, the empty punch, and more.

How to be a Master Instructor int the Martial Arts

(The original manual from The Master Instructor Course at MonsterMartialArts.) The only book of its kind in the world. Not an extreme boot camp kind of training manual, but the exact knowledge required to have perfect techniques and perfect form. The ability to get the idea from the instructor's head into the student's head. It can honestly be said that if you don't have the material in this book you aren't an instructor.

The Most Important Martial Arts Breakthrough in History

Matrix Karate

Five books detailing the entire system of Matrix Karate. This was the first course on Matrixing, and describes the procedure of matrixing. The system can be used as a template to matrix ANY other martial art.

The original book, on the original video course, was 160 pages. Thus, with over 650 pages, this series is an expanded viewpoint, answers more questions, gives more drills and techniques and exercises.

Matrix Karate, being scientifically designed, is not a style, it is a purity, and all other systems of Karate are substyles, or variations, of this one true Karate.

The Complete Series is available on Amazon.

The Universe of Al Case is Available at Amazon!

Discover unique worlds of imagination. Whole worlds of thought, unavailable to mankind, become known in these and other wondrous books. A more complete list of the works of Al Case may be found at:

AlCaseBooks.com

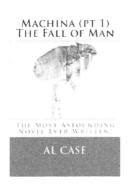

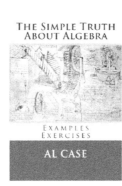

Made in the USA
Las Vegas, NV
08 October 2023

78758589R10066